Some Tanka in Thanks to Elroy, Not the Most Cantankerous Dog

poems by

Glenn D'Alessio

Finishing Line Press
Georgetown, Kentucky

Some Tanka in Thanks to Elroy, Not the Most Cantankerous Dog

Copyright © 2021 by Glenn D'Alessio
ISBN 978-1-64662-562-8 First Edition
All rights reserved under International and Pan-American Copyright Conventions. No part of this book may be reproduced in any manner whatsoever without written permission from the publisher, except in the case of brief quotations embodied in critical articles and reviews.

Note: "Tanka" in a section of poems below sometimes vary in syllable counts, just as they may in translations from Japanese to English, or English to Japanese.

The tanka is a thirty-one-syllable poem, traditionally written in a single unbroken line. A form of waka, Japanese song or verse, tanka translates as "short song," and is better known in its five-line, 5/7/5/7/7 syllable count form.

https://poets.org/glossary/tanka

Publisher: Leah Huete de Maines
FLP Editor: Christen Kincaid
Cover Painting and Photo: Glenn D'Alessio
Editing of Cover Photo of the Painting: John Hartman
Cover Design: Gail Heath
Editing to a number of poems: Susan Roney-O'Brien
Author Photo: Denise D'Alessio

Order online: www.finishinglinepress.com
also available on amazon.com

Author inquiries and mail orders:
Finishing Line Press
PO Box 1626
Georgetown, Kentucky 40324
USA

Table of Contents

Dogs and Cats

Size is Not How to Measure Him 1
To a Dog Person 2
Lost Dogs, The Way to World Peace 3
Dog Tricks Trainer 4
A Worcester State University Novelty 5

Tanka

Fooling Around 6
Aspects and Aspirations 7
Going Places 8
Almost Instinctive 9
Greenpeace, Walking Elroy 10

At Home

Do You Know 11
Getting it Right 12
I Need to Remember 13
Thinking of Him 14
Number One 15
Sinking In 16

Our Road Trip

My Ford Ranger in Memphis 17
The Seventy Mile-an-hour Bark in Live Oaks Florida 18
Torture 19

In the Fall and Winter of Our Lives

The Last Day of September, Interlude 20
Leaf Picking Out of the Sky 21
A New Meteor Shower 22
Lullaby to a Little Dog 23
In the Motion of Holding 24
Elroy Getting Brave 25
Abridged Nor'easter 26
Arctic Walk 27
Black Ice 28
After Sleeping Beauty 29
Elroy and I on a Midnight Walk 30

Postscript

A Beautiful Day to Be on the Roof 31

*To Denise, Gail, John, and Gracie, good friends of Elroy's,
and to the Second Chance Animal Shelter of East Brookfield,
Massachusetts; without which
we would have never been blessed by Elroy.*

Dogs and Cats

Size is Not How to Measure Him

How much grey matter
can fit in his exquisite head
doesn't matter in the presence of
a grey diamond between a Lone Ranger
mask of fur flanking his eyes,
when his breeding and temperament
couldn't be better,
from a shelter,
into our hearts.

To a Dog Person

This thing about Elroy
is that his claws
are not as pointed, sharp,
and hooked as a cat's,
yet he's just as soft
and agile, without
limbs that are hinged.

The thing about Elroy is
he's not so independent
to speak another language
and inhabit another world
like an alien who visits only
when engines are purring
or saucers flying with milk.

The thing is, even when wizened
with age, and jumping in sleep,
he's but a light nudge
away from the present,
and all attention
when we are demanding
a little understanding and love.

Lost Dogs, The Way to World Peace

They bring out the best in people
looking for Elroy
with black saddle bags on white,
and a star on his head,
losing his head, trotting away,
found at the Tower Hill School

while scores of good Samaritans
keep their eyes out for him,
taking my name and number,
until I see a woman walking him.
He's happy to be back,
smelling like her perfume.

Dog Tricks Trainer

Sit, Elroy, sit.
Sit and you can have this treat.
Sit.., sit.., sit....

Wait for a new command.
Sit.., sit.., sit....
This trick is boring.

Mark Isham is
playing cool jazz.
Sit, Elroy, sit.

I sit,
and know you can too.
So have this biscuit.

A Worcester State University Novelty

Adjunct instructors' first ever gifts
were business card cases
blue with W.S.U. white lettering
on cases big enough
to hold a few aspirin,
or better yet; as snuff boxes.

My wallet could hold more cards
and wouldn't be so easily lost; thus,
I almost tossed the W.S.U. tin in the garbage
after rejecting the idea to hide
a secret key in it for my son
or daughter to find after I die.

I can't imagine them finding my treasures
of value, like the metal coaster
with the 1964 New York World's Fair unisphere on it
that I gave to my parents 53 years ago,
good to them for collecting dust
on a top shelf above the sink,

but now I use it next to where I sit,
storing Elroy's dog treats,
until our new cat Mookie
keeps eating them,
so I keep some elsewhere
for Elroy who can't jump up there.

I put a few of his treats
in the W.S.U. snuff box
atop the World's Fair coaster,
for he's no novelty,
but should eat his treats
tossed whenever we please.

Tanka

Fooling Around

A Chair with a View

He's like Goldilocks.
Which chair will I sit on next,
is one softer,
or does another one have
a better view of the birds?

Brushing a Rat Terrier's Nose

Not batting an eye
his gait and gaze are straight ahead,
unperturbed by the
frog who whets his nose, knowing
a frog is not a rat.

Fooling With Elroy

He smiled and liked
what I was blowing at him,
dandelion fluff.
What can I do with him next?
He prefers to lead the fool.

All Yours in the Town of Warren

I found a dog bone
in my pocket. Who is it for,
Elroy? Is it yours?
After giving it to you
you took it to Warren.

Aspects and Aspirations

Where is Elmo?

Elroy, where are you?
I like a large audience
and you have a large
desire for walks and friendship,
at the window when I go.

Looking Up to Elroy

I look up to you
with your paws high on my chest.
You're not a lap dog.
Your head is higher than mine.
Many things make you happy.

His Nose

Sticks out from under
the crinkled covers, a-quiver,
his nose boiling things down
and solving clues of existence,
remaining cool. His nose knows all.

A Taste of Freedom

He would rather sit
in the June sun watching koi,
and taste his freedom,
than sit on the rocker where
I play with words in the shade.

Going Places

July 14, 2016

Moths and mosquitos,
flocks of them walking the dog.
Elroy doesn't mind.
For trees, it'll be a bad year,
caterpillars eating them.

How Poetic?

Yesterday a worm,
today a salamander.
She was neon red,
safely picked up from the road
when Elroy and I were walking.

In the Rain

Up and down the street
that not good enough for him,
turned to down and up,
and still he didn't lift his leg,
slopping through more for him to rain.

Forms of Flow

The water flowing
by the four corners, pancaked
from upstream black and
silver snakes and ribbons
Elroy's feet made rivulets in.

From Luck to Yuck

Prancing through deep snow
we came to a sandy road
of slush arresting flakes
so Elroy tested his paws
and we slowed down in the cold.

Almost Instinctive

Your Digs

Digging to China,
or are you fluffing your nest,
your paws going fast
in my bed. Want a shovel –
duller than your claws, I hope.

The Frequent Flyer

He's curled up with
a bony wing of a leg
over his nose
before he goes for a walk,
his time to perk up and fly.

Doldrums in the Dark

The air doesn't move.
The moon appears just as still
baking in the sun,
mosquitos and I languid.
Elroy smiles and lifts his leg.

Behind Gail's Pond

Is watching her fish,
more contagious, Elroy,
than our taking naps is?
Koi pond's water falls, dragon flies
fly, and birds splash in their baths.

Greenpeace, Walking Elroy

I like Greenpeace, but
their renewal envelope
is my fly swatter
directly from my mail box
to my face, glasses off.

Their supplications
and stories are stiff enough
to swat cheeks and neck –
a bloody environment.
At least I'm not hunting whales.

At Home

Do You Know?

Do you know we have
a happy dog?

When there's nothing to beg for,
or reason to go out,

he's not barking, but smiling,
and then dreaming,

feet to the front
curled and ready to fly.

Getting it Right

It's a most serious business
to hug and pet Elroy
who does not protest
but is open for more,

even in his sleep.
My business being
to follow the softest
directions of his fur.

I Need to Remember

I need to remember
to take dog biscuits
out of my shirt pocket
before I do laundry.
I need to remember to stop
during our walks
and give Elroy a pat.

Elroy needs to guess
which hand I have a biscuit in.
And with my sleight of hand
his memory is no good for guessing.
But does this matter?
I keep biscuits in my breast pocket.
This he never forgets.

He should do my laundry.

Thinking of Him

Thinking of him makes me smile
like the mystery of bed covers
mounded high,

or a triangular expression
with a diamond on his head
looking out the window

when I wave and blow my horn,
thinking he likes that
as much as I like

being tickled when he wriggles in,
fickle for flicking the covers
over his burrow in my bed.

Number One

I said to him, "there is only one,"
and with his teeth and tongue,
he bit into it, not knowing
the difference between one and two.

But guilty in knowing,
I gave him biscuit two,
and just as quickly
two turned into one.

Sinking In

Between the back of the
couch cushions
Elroy slowly sinks in,

claws scraping,
and legs extended
into a chasm for dreams

and stuffy air, where
only his nose and tail
poke into the open.

Our Road Trip

My Ford Ranger in Memphis

My pickup truck makes Elroy and I
shake, rattle, and roll.

I feel like Elvis,
only it isn't a hotrod.

But with no air conditioning
I too am rocking hot.

The Seventy Mile-an-hour Bark in Live Oaks Florida

We aren't moving.
That seems to be the trouble—
not moving fast enough.

We need to roll as fast as
"bark bark," bounce bounce
with his every ounce.

Torture

My name is Elroy.
A piece of meat fell between
the seats. I smell it.

In the Fall and Winter of Our Lives

The Last Day of September, Interlude

There couldn't be a nicer day;
fallen leaves skipping over stones
like brushes on cymbals
when I take an apple from the tree,

and take a poem
from the apple's shadows
stirring leafy filters,
sun matting all that's happening.

Elroy sleeping on my lap
has an ideal temperature,
almost no panting,
yet adding form to my writing,

inviting me
to skip work,
letting my idle eyes
follow a sulfur moth,

Elroy surveying the scene
with the knowledge of his nose
until I resolve
to go back to work.

Leaf Picking Out of the Sky

They fall, and I need to fly,
      jumping across the road
      to stab erratic paths

of wind born yellow birch leaves
      and others, like stones to miss,
       wishing to catch them when they dodge,

until my little dog Elroy
      sniffing markings dogs lifted,
      makes a basket catch upon his back.

A New Meteor Shower

Coming and going,
the canopy's thickness
plays tricks with my
careening neck,
peering between leaves
for shooting stars,

when the stars I see
seem to hover,
and are shooting from
so far away
they are standing still
from my perspective,

so much higher than
my rat terrier, Elroy,
who offers no opinion
beside my feet,
preserving my belief
that as still as we are standing

we are spinning
faster than the wind
through the eyes of the canopy
that is moving as much
as the meteors
not seen tonight.

Lullaby to a Little Dog

Little Dog
little dog with the long legs,
all zonked out
when it's time for bed.

Little dog
little dog
in the middle of bed
blinking your eyes,

you're a little dog
proud of your role,
rolling under covers
where you never snore,

sure of your place
beside me,
soft and warm,
warm and soft.

In the Motion of Holding

Your legs and feet to toes
slip through the holes my fingers make
when silk springs to my resistance.

I preen and pet,
betting you'll stay
to dream and breathe

grass is high,
rabbit fast,
but your path better

until her hopping
reaches the wind,
and she springs wings.

Then you stop your trot,
hold up a paw
and sniff the wind

bewitching you
to lay down and sleep.
Pleasing me to keep petting you.

Elroy Getting Brave

Everything spattered.
Pond in tatters.

Drops jumping into sheets
of angles fleeting

in our compass readings –
southern slants

to northern drives
missing us.

Elroy becoming brave
between the beats

until ribbons of mist
began hitting us

getting soaked
in our shelter.

Abridged Nor'easter

Out with Elroy, our walk was abridged
by branches blowing out of the sky
with their stories to tell
louder than I yell,
"I didn't see it coming,"

hunched forward under a poncho,
debris everywhere
punctuating our steps
in haste, imagining the ending—
dynamite crack and silence.

Arctic Walk

Gay in his gait
walking up Griffing Road
packed with snow,
his nose short circuiting
his nerves only lasting so long,
four above zero clipping his will,
until his feet need oil
and the creaking begins,
elastics snapping back
like an old wooden toy
fracturing his stride,
trying to walk on air,
slow motioned
like a bird going down.

Black Ice

Black Ice in ribbons
magically swallows light,

carving the
surface glaze

of roads unsafely
crazed for us to fall

and be immobilized
like winter snows that no longer blow,

granulized with age,
senselessly dense and dirty,

offering trash
lifted from drifts

like Elroy lifts his leg
to all things worthy

like archeological digs,
decomposing them further

from matrices of crystals
and artifacts alike.

After Sleeping Beauty

> *a bony lungfish caught by a kiss,*
> *I was hauled in from sleep's unfathoming depths*
> *to another life, where the scales worked in gold*
>   "Sleeping Beauty" – Debora Greger

Sleeping Beauty, awakened by a kiss
became old, and lost hold
of youthful beauty,

but this did not bring the brothers Grimm,
no longer feeling the cold after
the Prince moved on so long ago.

The sun was in her face.
Walking briskly with her terrier
who had grown just as old.

Elroy and I on a Midnight Walk

The moon casts shadows
through the trees
blueing the pavement
between smooth light

as we move deeper
into the forest coolness
clutching us closely
and shaping our dreams.

Elroy sniffs one way
and I drift like smoke
into a thickening border
of growing stone walls

and banks harboring
wind rows of trees
obliterating the brightest
moon light.

Postscript

A Beautiful Day to Be on the Roof

1.

The trees sway my way,
some blue peaking through
but no sun, and no rain.

Red oak leaf fingers
supplicating me from twenty-feet
to give them hugs

but I stay away,
having no sails,
concerned for branches stripped bare,

not fair if caterpillars starve,
but they'll also starve
if they defoliate more forest.

Other trees made the rafters I sit atop,
so I forget these thoughts, flashing the chimney,
and dragging a tarp across my shirt

smudging tar over yellow plaid,
glad to be above my second floor's attic
that will be cooler after cutting a ridge vent into it,

finally willing to clapboard over
less effective gable vents
a squirrel once chewed holes through.

I feel like a squirrel,
looking down into the forest

where I buried Elroy three days ago.

He was so much more than a nut.
Can he fly now?
I almost wish to test my wings,

knowing falling on my head
would be the only way
I could grow some.

2.

The daisies in my lawn
or daisies instead of lawn, I admire,
just as I do the mountain laurel
and rhododendron
below my house.

Also lucky for the rabbit
passing through my garden
that I'm not a hawk,
and that he didn't eat
the bush beans and squash coming up

or I would have acted hungry
even if I had fed him carrots
last winter
when I thought
he should have been hibernating.

Elroy is no longer here.
But I'm glad his friend the rabbit is.
At least I think they were friends
since when they were nose to nose
Elroy didn't eat him.

Glenn D'Alessio lives in West Brookfield, MA with his wife. His first class in poetry was taken at North Country Community College in Saranac Lake, NY. It focused on the beats. Much more valuable to Glenn was a class about short stories by Patricia Wiley. He also adopted his first dog, Seico, then. She was a white dog with a ring around one eye and her tail. During 1971 the two of them spent summer in a homemade lean-to at Caulkin's Creek in the Adirondacks. He has never been without a dog since.

One of Glenn's most productive periods of writing was last decade. Elroy deserves credit. "My Hero// My Hero cheers me whenever I come Home/ from whatever day's stressful complaints/ and paints me an alternative universe/ of tranquil seas and gentle breeze/ so our hearts will ease."

For a small rat terrier, Elroy was fearless of any dog or person, regardless to size, and was most gregarious. There was only one exception. "Cameras// Elroy was from/ one of those cultures/ whose soul would be/ snared by a camera's// shutter grabbing/ feet or eyes,/ so his would go/ to Elysian fields,// or toward the nearest/ inanimate/ couch or table,/ both totems to protect// his curly tail/ late behind him,/ not wanting to become/ locked into a box." This phobia was like Glenn's childhood worry that something would sneak up behind him. That's why he would circle to unwind himself on landings, and at the tops to stairs. In doing this he could see what was behind—his winding like Elroy's tail.

They were both cantankerous, but on a midnight walk in starlight or first thing in the morning they would strike a balance. Elroy would be on a leash so he wouldn't get lost and die. Thus, Glenn considered a little restraint to be for Elroy a "Freedom of the Leash// He pulls and I push./ I'm small, trotting to his walking,/ and I'm in no rush/ when he has to go to work./ We find a happy medium." The two of them were like a match made in heaven.

www.ingramcontent.com/pod-product-compliance
Lightning Source LLC
LaVergne TN
LVHW041603070426
835507LV00011B/1290